F.U.C.K.

YOUR INSECURITIES!

THE NO-BULLSHIT GUIDE TO
STOP DOUBTING YOURSELF,
BE WHO YOU ARE, AND DO
WHAT YOU WANT

DEANTE YOUNG

DIRTYTRUTH
PUBLISHING

ISBN: 978-1-7369466-0-2

Dedicated to my Ma, Deborah, my Grandma, Elizabeth, and my daughters Desiree and Kayla. You have given me blessings in life that no one else ever has. I love you all!
–D.Y.

TABLE OF CONTENTS

"The reason we struggle with insecurity is because we compare our behind-the-scenes with everyone else's highlight reel."

–Steven Furtick

INTRODUCTION

Everyone on planet earth has insecurities, and they will kick your ass and ruin your life if you let them. The worst part is that they hold you back and stop you from accomplishing some of the most important shit of your life.

Insecurities create self-doubt, which makes you question your worthiness, envy other people, and just flat out believe that you're not good enough for this job, that relationship, or that awesome opportunity.

When is the last time that you truly believed you could accomplish anything you wanted to? No matter how hard you try, you can't seem to get it through your head you are more than good enough to do whatever the fuck you want.

The world will have you feeling inferior if you don't have this body type or that college degree or possess this specific skill, so through all that, you're thinking, "There's no use in trying anything, right?"

No. You're as wrong about yourself as America was about Bill Cosby! *F.U.C.K. Your Insecurities* is a masterclass designed to help you out of your hellhole of limiting beliefs by proving to yourself that you've always been a kickass muthafucka who is good enough for anything you want in life.

No more playing small or letting society dictate how you should feel about yourself. No more being envious because of what other people have because you'll realize how goddamn lucky you are to have what YOU have.

In this book, you will learn several key things:

- The one thing you need that is far more important than confidence to succeed.

- Why people you think are better than you actually admire the hell out of you.

- The four-step process of handling your insecurities and make them irrelevant.

- How to write the ultimate love letter to yourself.

- Why your biggest inspiration should be your infant self.

- How to turn your "shortcomings" into your ultimate weapon.

- And much more!

I can't count the number of times that my insecurities tossed me around like a rag doll and made me feel about as useful as a sailboat in the desert. In grade school, I was ridiculed for having a waistline as wide as the equator—

in middle school, I was humiliated for not wearing brand name sneakers, and in high school, I had a better chance of beating Mike Tyson in a boxing ring than getting a girl to kiss me.

I've been considered "the elephant in the room" because my weight total looks more like a social security number. I've been ridiculed for having a ding-a-ling that's shorter than an earring, and I've been called every derogatory name in the book for being black, fat, broke, obscene, and damn near every other "undesirable" quality.

In other words, I know what having limiting beliefs, self-doubt, and a truckload of insecurities is all about. But I wouldn't trade any of my life experiences for anything, and it's because of all that shit that I've grown through that makes me believe that I'm the only person on this planet most qualified to coach you on handling your insecurities.

In reading through this book, you will have a much better understanding of your value and impact in the world. You will view some of the worst and most challenging times of your life to be essential resources in your future success. You will also realize that there's never a reason to want anyone else's life more than your own.

As long as you read this book with an open mind and actually take part in the writing prompts and suggestions, I pinky promise that you will never allow your insecurities and self-doubt to push you around ever again. Your huge goals won't happen overnight, but you will see immediate changes in your attitude and self-belief as long as you take this information seriously and implement it.

Don't drag your feet and procrastinate. Read this book with purpose and intent so that you can maximize all the mindset-shifting gold that you now have in your possession. Let's get to the business of stepping into who you were always meant to be but never realized it.

Until now.

PART I:
THESE ASSHOLES ARE
BRAINWASHING YOU

"When a child is learning to walk and falls down 50 times, they never think to themselves, "Maybe this isn't for me."

—the unknown diary

BABIES MAKE YOU LOOK PATHETIC

Insecurities come from slow and methodical brainwashing by the piece of shit mass media and the general public. Long before we are born, society has already decided what's considered good, bad, beautiful, ugly, luxurious, raggedy, desirable, and undesirable.

Before we even show up in a damn ultrasound picture, standards have been decided on what we should be embarrassed about or proud of. This fucked up shit affects every person in the world with the exception of one specific group: Babies.

There's no question that babies are the most self-assured people on the planet. Every baby I have ever seen has always acted as if they had no fucks to give about anything.

You've seen that shit too. Babies usually learn how to walk sometime around their first birthday. They'll walk around completely naked, covered in food, or screaming their fucking head off without a care in the world—even if they are in a room full of people.

Baby boys never give a shit who sees their ding-a-ling—even if it's as tiny as a damn Tic Tac. Baby girls don't care who sees their undeveloped chest, and neither gender would be fazed by someone telling them they are ugly. That amazing attitude makes you look pathetic because all that shit would hurt your feelings.

INCREDIBLE SELF-BELIEF

The first year of a baby's life is filled with trying, failing, believing in themselves, not caring what other people say to them, and flat out doing what the fuck they want. When my daughters started crawling, they'd crawl to a chair, table, or any other object and pull themselves up. If they were in danger, I'd tell them to stop or pull them away.

They went right back to doing the same exact thing in every situation, and it became obvious why almost all babies are so damn resilient and headstrong. They haven't yet been brainwashed by the world and made to feel mediocre, worthless, inadequate, or insecure. They have incredible self-belief.

My first feelings of insecurity started when I was four years old. I was in Child Development class, and we often played that bullshit game Duck, Duck, Goose. Every kid in my class was skinny as hell, and whenever they got to me, I was the "goose!"

This was devastating for me, chubby as I was, having to chase around the skinny kid. I never understood until recently why they almost always picked me as the goose. Then it dawned on me that if someone is chasing you, you hope that person is slow. Obviously, being "heavy" was not acceptable, and kids would soon make it clear to me if I didn't know it already. How much time between being a baby with no fucks to give to feeling like I wasn't as good as the "normal" sized kids?

Three measly years!

Socializing with other kids started a downward spiral from which I couldn't recover. As a baby and toddler, I didn't have any insecurities other than a fear of someone not hearing me cry if I needed something (I'm assuming).

DIG DEEP TO RECALL YOUR TURNING POINT

Your insecurities may have begun earlier than mine, or they could've been later. But whatever the case, you need to do a little mental digging into your past to figure out when you reached your "turning point." That's when the bottom fell out of your "no fucks given" mindset, and insecurities began growing inside you.

Of course, insecurities come in all shapes, sizes, and types. For me, it was the status of my waistline more than anything else that "stole my joy." I've seen people become insecure because of their lack of finances, a disability, some undesirable quality, and a whole bunch of other shit.

Knowing when you went from that carefree baby to the kid (or adult) that was insecure is super important because you're trying to get to know yourself better. We think we know ourselves, but you'd be surprised to find out that there's a lot we don't know at all.

It took me until a couple of years ago to learn very important information about myself, and it's helped so much that I decided to write a book to help as many people as I can.

Identify Your Self-Doubts

Your first couple of years on earth were an amazing time in your life. You were at your most fearless and self-assured until the world started to inflict its opinions, standards, and biases on you. Because of that, you can't unlearn what you've been taught, and you can't simply erase your insecurities.

But you can recapture your baby magic of "no fucks given" by shifting your perspective on things. Something that I've found to be highly effective is giving myself a reality check and identifying my self-doubts, which requires you to become very self-aware.

What are the things you believe that you can't do, are not good enough for, or will never have (that you actually want)? Make a list of them on paper or in a "notes" app on your mobile device. This is important because you will gain clarity by doing this, as long as you are brutally honest with your answers.

When it comes to other people, you don't necessarily have to *care* what they think of you, but you should at least be *aware* of what they think. That gives you the upper hand in social situations because you won't delude yourself about how you're seen and perceived.

Then, learn what things about you are considered undesirable by the general public, which I call "visual and social abnormalities." Society tends to favor what's considered "normal" and "standard," which also happens to be familiar to most people.

What Doesn't Define You Can't Hurt You

Using an unemployed drunk as a social example, if that person were around the general public, there would be glares, whispers, and yes—laughter and annoyance. I actually knew a guy like that, and people treated him like a second-class citizen because of how socially off-putting he was. He seemed to have zero self-awareness which is a terrible position in which to be.

Using myself as a visual example, I know being hundreds and hundreds of pounds overweight is abnormal. You are less likely to encounter a 1000 pound person in public, and even though it can happen—it's not likely. So, my self-awareness makes me realize that I'll be looked at and perceived in negative ways by some people.

Because my waistline doesn't define me or illustrate what I am capable of, I can live with being "overcaloried." Everyone has at least one "visual or socially undesirable" quality, but if it doesn't define you, it can't hurt you.

It reminds me of a song by Eminem featuring Dr. Dre on *The Eminem Show* album. The song, "Say What You Say" is meant to be a diss track towards music producer Jermaine Dupri. Dre made many unflattering comments about Dupri, and repeatedly ridiculed his height.

When Dupri was asked what he thought about Dre's attempt at humiliation, he issued a simple yet fascinating response. "All he said is that I'm short," said Dupri as he shrugged his shoulders as if to say, "What's your point?"

Dupri's answer proved that he was self-aware that he is a short man, and he knows that his height is irrelevant because his success as a producer is massive, and his life seems to be awesome. Whatever your insecurities are, they can't make you less of a person if you don't allow that nonsense to happen.

KEEP IN MIND

- The world and the general public are always trying to brainwash you about what's good and what's not. Don't let it affect your thinking.

- Babies are the most self-assured people because they haven't been tainted by the opinions and standards of the world.

- Dig deep to recall when your "turning point" took place. That's when you went from a self-assured baby to having a growing list of insecurities.

- Identify your self-doubts and write down the things that you are insecure about.

- What doesn't define you can't hurt you no matter how embarrassing the insecurity is.

"Everybody knows someone like that: wonderful, attractive people full of passion and ideals. You envy them, but you know there's a dark side, which is brutal and cruel and violent. That dark side informs what's wonderful about them, and the passion and rage inform the darkness; they're inseparable."

–David Thewlis

A Rolls Royce Has the Same Problems as a Ford Focus

Some people are more in shape than you, have more money than you, drive a more expensive car, live in a better house, are smarter and more successful—but they are not better than you. The dirty truth is simple: everyone has problems and insecurities because they are human. Never put anyone on a pedestal because no one deserves that.

Take one look at Beyoncé and JAY-Z. They are global superstars and a married couple with three healthy children and a combined net worth reaching into the billions. Their careers include legendary moments, chart-topping dominance, and enough awards to fill a museum.

Their cultural influence has been about as mind-boggling as a blindfolded trip on a goddamn roller coaster. And even with all of that luxury, achievement, and privilege, those muthafuckas have the same damn problems as the rest of us. Consider them a pair of expensive ass Rolls Royces. Consider us to be an affordable Ford Focus.

The point here is simple as shit. Just because something or someone is considered high class or holds high status doesn't mean that it (or them) is immune from the same crap that everything or everyone else is.

ENVY NO ONE—NOT EVEN THE RICH AND FAMOUS

In the Beyoncé and JAY-Z example I presented, they are so accomplished in their fields and are the envy of many people. But guess what? They have insecurities that you wouldn't believe. They suffer through the same emotions as the rest of us, whether it's pain, frustration, self-doubt, fear—you name it.

Let's not forget the gut-punch their marriage suffered a few years ago. Back when Jay fucked "Becky with the good hair" even though he was married to the almighty Queen Bey!

Let's not forget how scandalous it all became when a very pissed-off Beyonce released her *Lemonade* album and the vindictive short films that came along with it.

Let's not forget JAY-Z pouring his soul into several songs from this *4:44* album and the vulnerability he showed that I had never seen from him. After all, he is the same guy who made the club hit song, "Big Pimpin'," in which he eloquently states:

"I'm a pimp in every sense of the word, bitch
Better trust than believe 'em
In the cut where I keep 'em
'Til I need a nut, 'til I need to beat the guts
Then it's, beep beep and I'm pickin' 'em up
Let 'em play with the dick in the truck"

I know that he made that song eons ago, way back in 1999 when he was a young and swaggering mover and shaker on the rise. But his level of focus and ambition has probably never been matched by anyone in the hip hop game—and rarely in any industry outside it.

But that's the point of all this. JAY-Z represents the absolute height of living the American Dream. He is the epitome of success, and the fact that he was even in the position to date Beyoncé, let alone marry her and squirt a bunch of kids into her, is further evidence of his uncommon success.

Yet he still fell short as a man, not my words, but his. He still has his blind spots. The world is in the palm of his hands and has been for a long time, yet he still proves how unremarkable he is as a human.

THE BULLSHIT THAT THE WORLD TELLS YOU

The world will have you believe that if you are as physically attractive as Beyoncé, you are a commodity and ideal in your beauty. The world portrays the usual standards of physical attractiveness in a way that suggests that anyone who possesses it is above being cheated on. Tell that horseshit to Beyoncé, Halle Berry, and millions of regular women who are about as fine as a pair of diamonds wrapped in hundred dollar bills but were still victims of infidelity.

This is the same BS that goes on with material stuff too.

I'm reminded of the years that I was contracted with a sales organization, and every manager at the place made it a point to drive high-end cars. The agency's co-owner was the proverbial granddaddy of 'em all because he was pushing a fucking Rolls Royce.

At the time, I had a nearly decade-old Chrysler, but the muthafucka made me happy. The management team's parking lot was treated like a Hollywood red carpet! The Rolls, the Bentley, the Range Rover, the Ferrari, the Porsche, yada yada yada.

People fawned over those "baller ass cars" because most of us had only seen that shit on television. I was one of the people sucked in the first year of being there.

At some point, I realized that my trusty Chrysler managed to get me to the office every day and everywhere else I needed to go. The Rolls Royce guy also managed to get to the office, which means that we both arrived at the same place even though his car's price tag was $300-400K easily. My car was a meager 14 grand by comparison.

I get it. He was a multi-millionaire, and I was lucky to come away with enough money to finance my Doritos habit, so we were not in the same boat. But I'm not drawing that picture; I'm drawing this one: the most important thing we need a car to do for us is get us to our destinations.

In that way, the Rolls was no better than my Chrysler. The Rolls needed oil and gasoline to run, could get flat tires, and could be destroyed if it were in an accident.

People are the same way, so there's never a good reason to act as though anyone is better than you because they have a six-pack, or long hair or a huge cock (guy), or a rack so stacked under their blouse (gal) that you might lose your mind if she were to release those suckers from captivity.

"Don't be impressed by money, power, degrees and looks. Be impressed by generosity, integrity, humility and kindness."

–Lewis Howes, New York Times Bestselling Author, multimillionaire entrepreneur

MATERIAL THINGS AND PHYSICAL ATTRACTIVENESS ARE MISLEADING

I needed someone to explain this philosophy to me when I was a young fucker with low self-esteem. I always believed that guys were better than me because they were skinny, and society had already proven to me that it favors non-fat folks.

Because of the mass media, our perception of acceptable and unacceptable, and desirable and undesirable, is fucked up. On the covers of almost every magazine, the vast majority of female celebrities are razor-thin, and their face glows with airbrushed perfection.

Male celebrities have either been boyishly handsome, such as a young Leo DiCaprio, or ruggedly gorgeous, such as Sylvester Stallone or Bruce Willis. Film and television rarely produced shows with fat people in lead roles, and if they were in a movie or show, they tended to be portrayed as a novelty.

Just another punchline.

With all of that serving as the standard of awesomeness in this country, how could any of us not feel insecure? And if television wasn't enough to push you over the edge, your friends and associates definitely could.

Have you ever felt insecure about getting hired for a job that you really wanted? Trust me, that's a common emotion in that situation, so I advise you to embrace it. There is something very important to remember: the people in the same position you want have flaws and shortcomings.

We just have a dumb habit of putting people on a pedestal that have something or some quality that we wish we had. I've had candid conversations with homeless alcoholics, and I've had similar conversations with millionaires.

I discovered that people from drastically different social classes are closer to being the same than being different from each other. Both types of people had an addiction to alcohol or drugs and could be cruel, self-centered, and obnoxious. Millionaires are no different than other people just because they have a bunch of money.

If they are different, it is because of their natural character, not their expensive shit. A handsome asshole in a $5,000 suit is the same as a wrinkle-faced asshole in $10 overalls, proving that money and physical attractiveness are misleading as hell. And guess what? I've been around both types of people, and both are full of self-doubt!

This is all great news for the insecurities you have. It illustrates an often unnoticed truth about people that you perceive to be "above" you. They had their moments of insecurity just like you and are guaranteed to have them still.

No one ever gets to the point of not having any insecurities. So keep that in mind the next time you feel intimidated around anyone, whether you're interviewing for a job or hitting on someone.

KEEP IN MIND

- The people who have better looks, more money, and nicer things are still no better than you are.

- JAY-Z and Beyonce are billionaire superstars who still experience the same issues as the rest of us. Don't envy anyone—including famous people.

- The world will have you believe that having an expensive car or some other "desirable" thing or physical quality makes you better than others. It's all a lie because a Rolls Royce has the same problems as a Ford Focus.

- Don't be impressed by tangible things like money and power. Be impressed with the truly meaningful things such as humility and generosity.

- A handsome asshole in a $5,000 suit is the same as a wrinkle-faced asshole in $10 overalls, and they are both filled with self-doubt.

- No one ever gets to the point of not having insecurities. Keep that in mind the next time you are intimidated by a person or opportunity that you perceive to be out of your reach.

"Life can only be understood backwards;
But it must be lived forwards."

–Soren Kierkegaard

5 LIFE LESSONS THAT WILL MAKE YOU A BAD ASS

Damn near every person I know bitches about their problems. "Today sucked," they often say. The average person plays victim better than Nicole Brown Simpson, who actually was a victim.

Here's a secret: if you start looking at your life experiences as teaching tools for handling insecurities instead of one horrible moment after another, you'll be amazed at how much better things get. And here's the best part— they don't actually get better; your damn perspective just changes.

I can't stand the fuckers who find problems in every opportunity instead of the other way around. The second you understand that shit happens **for** you and not to you, doors will mysteriously open up like a scary-ass haunted house.

Take me, for instance. The first "raw deal" that life threw at me was giving me a semen donor for a father who was not much different than a goddamn bartender at the end of his shift. He poured the liquid then took his ass home.

Use these five experiences from my life to help smother your self-doubt and insecurities to become a badass!

1. Never Seek Anyone's Approval

Halfway through seventh grade, this smug son of a bitch in my class made a public spectacle out of me by poking fun at my shoes. These were the days that Nikes and Air Jordan's were becoming status symbols for young urban kids, and I failed to get the memo.

I was wearing a pair of off-brand bowling shoes, and I got roasted like a case of peanuts for that ill-advised choice. Kids laughed their asses off, which sent me home begging my mom to buy me a pair of Nike sneakers. When I showed up the next day, I couldn't wait for that jerk kid to see my new name-brand shoes and be impressed.

When I pointed out the shoes to him, he was completely withdrawn and had almost no reaction. I felt like the village idiot because I stressed over getting approval from him. I never got that shit, and I was crushed.

Your Takeaway

- If you're ever in a situation in which you seek someone's approval about your appearance, your lifestyle, or anything else—snap out of that bullshit thought process.

- It is an absolutely unfulfilling journey trying to gain acceptance from another person. All they have are opinions about you, and who gives a shit about theirs? Think of it this way, if one person praises you for something, you'll probably feel good about yourself. But the next person could erase all that sunshine and rainbows by criticizing that thing the first person liked. This is exactly why you need to remember that your life and its details do not require approval.

2. BE YOURSELF NO MATTER WHO DOESN'T LIKE IT

During the summer after my freshman year in high school, I was desperate for a girlfriend. Ridiculously, I asked a guy friend for the phone number of a girl that we both knew, but he was friendly with her. I proceeded to call her and pretend that I was him because I knew she had a crush on him, and I believed she would never give me the time of day.

We spoke on the phone for a couple of weeks. Despite her repeated questioning about why my voice sounded different on the phone, I convinced her to meet me at the mall. I was scared as hell of how she would react when she realized I was not who she thought she was talking to.

When we saw each other, she was pissed, but she "allowed" me to pay for her ticket to see a movie with me.

Nothing good ever came from my deception, which was fueled by my massive insecurities.

Your Takeaway

- I know for sure that if your insecurities cause you to believe that you can't be your true and authentic self, then you are disrespecting the fuck out of yourself by pretending to be someone else.

- No person, place, or thing is worth diminishing your specialness as an individual to do such a crazy thing. Even if you managed to get away with fooling someone by pretending to be someone else, it is a fool's errand, and you will live to regret it. Be in love with being you and to hell with whoever doesn't like it.

3. Never Dim Your Light While Making Someone Else's Bright

When I was 16, I was so damn happy that I met a girl over the phone who seemed to like me as much as I liked her. With this being the early 1990s, I asked her to send me a picture of her in the mail, and when I received it—I thought she was really cute. When she asked me to return the favor and send one of myself, I panicked more than O.J. did when the cops found blood from the victims in his driveway.

Because I was incredibly insecure about my physical appearance, I believed that a photo of myself would cause this girl to stop talking to me on the phone and never want to meet me in person. I sent her pictures of my cousin and two of my guy friends because I knew that girls always liked them. When she received the pictures, she told me that me and my "friends are hot."

She then asked which of the guys was me. It was a simple question, yet it overwhelmed me. I admitted that none of the photos were of me while heaping praise on my cousin and friends. I talked about how studly they were and how her other friends would really dig them, all of which made her more confused about why I didn't include photos of myself. If you are guilty of this sort of bullshit behavior, I'm begging you to throw that shit in the garbage.

Your Takeaway

- There's nothing wrong with saying good things about friends, family, or anyone else. But elevating others while dimming your own light is a disgusting practice and just leads to more insecurity. The dirty truth is simple: no matter how awesome you think someone else is, they never quite think that way about themselves.

- Remember, we tend to be our own worst enemy, and those who we put in the spotlight are just as insecure as we are, maybe in different ways or even in similar ways. And this doesn't only apply to dating or sex; it applies to any area of life. Don't shine bright lights on a co-worker and downplay yourself—I've done that crap too, and it was dumb. You're better than that.

4. One Monkey Don't Stop No Show

My aunt had the remarkable skill of making the most amazing spaghetti I'd ever tasted. When I was 17, she asked me to babysit her children while she was at work. I agreed and soon found a pot of deliciousness on her stove. Long story short, I devoured far more of that yumminess than was acceptable to her.

When my aunt found out, she laid into me like an abusive husband on a bender. I later told my grandmother of the humiliating experience, and she was beyond pissed off.

Within moments, she handed me money and told my mother to go to the store to buy all the ingredients to make a pot of spaghetti for me to have all to myself. I was shocked at how mad my grandmother was at her daughter—my aunt—for scolding me about the spaghetti.

"One monkey don't stop no show," she said to me, almost like a rallying cry. Yes, she was talking about food, but the moment stood out to me so much that I continue to hold it close and apply it to all aspects of life.

Your Takeaway

- The message that "one monkey don't stop no show" teaches the idea that the world is full of opportunities far and wide, so you should never fawn over any particular one.

- When you believe that a person, job, or any other opportunity is the "only show in town," it causes you to operate from a place of desperation and insecurity.

- But when you operate with the mindset that there's an abundance of whatever you didn't get from one person or one place, you will realize that there's always plenty more where that came from. Get in the practice of thinking that way, and you'll be unstoppable!

5. Never Be Starstruck By Anyone

I had the opportunity to take a girl that I badly wanted (to fuck) out for a night of fun. I was less than two months from my 20th birthday, and I still had a hell of a lot to learn. It felt like a damn miracle that this particular chick allowed me to hang out with her that night because I had put her on a pedestal as soon as I met her months earlier. She was slim, petite, and cute, and that combination made her feel like she was out of my league.

When I picked her up that night, I was shocked when she told me that she intended to have sex with me. She repeatedly flirted as I drove and made it very clear that she was feeling frisky, which made me nervous as hell. I now realize it's because I didn't feel worthy of this girl; why would a slender beauty go for a fat fuck like me? If you've ever thought of someone or something as too glorious or too off-limits for you, stop that fawning adulation right fucking now!

Your Takeaway

- A huge part of feeling insecure comes from making that thing or person 100 feet tall in your mind. Imagine thinking of a great job opportunity as being the most amazing thing you could ever get.

- The more you obsess over it and view it in your mind as a once-in-a-lifetime privilege, the more you risk feeling as though you don't deserve it.

- The same thing applies to dating someone that you perceive as being above you in quality or standards. The key to overcoming that unnecessary adulation of people and things is to get it in your mind that they are never worth all that mental energy. Best advice? Kill the fanfare, and you will begin to realize that nothing and no one is too good for you!

KEEP IN MIND

- Never seek anyone's approval for any aspect of your life. Advice or opinions are fine but looking to others for their "blessing" or acceptance is an unfulfilling journey that you will ultimately regret.

- Be yourself no matter who doesn't like it. You are an original, and no one has the right to try to make you something that you're not. If you do that to yourself, you are disrespecting your own specialness.

- Don't dim your light while making someone else's bright. It's okay to give people their props and praise, but don't put yourself in the "shit house" while putting them in the "penthouse!" You bring awesome stuff to the table just as they do.

- Never forget that "one monkey don't stop no show." No one and nothing is so goddamn exclusive that you should fawn over it or them like a shameless lapdog. The sooner you understand that there is an unlimited abundance of anything you could ever want, the better your life will become.

- Never be starstruck by anyone. Physical attractiveness comes a dime a dozen, and so does almost everything else that is superficial. Stop making someone else's head expand with your admiration of them and treat them like the "standard" people that they are.

"Dear haters, I couldn't help but notice that awesome ends with 'me' and ugly starts with 'u.'"

–Saima Khatri

YOUR SECRET ADMIRERS (HATERS) ALREADY KNOW YOU'RE THE SHIT

By now, it should be clear that we all have insecurities. One thing might not be so obvious; we also possess many things that we take for granted that others wish they had as their reality. Legendary motivational speaker Les Brown once said, "It's hard to see the whole picture when you're in the frame." The point is your haters are actually secret admirers. Even friends and acquaintances tend to admire and envy things about you and often recognize great or awesome qualities that went clear over your head.

Years ago, I hosted and produced a controversial web series that earned as much praise as it did criticism. During the show's third season, an attractive young woman sought me out and quickly became my trusted assistant.

She was fawned over by a series of lapdogs—I mean, guys, and to be honest, I also felt that she was a tasty treat. Deep down, I didn't fully believe I could score action with her, yet other dudes believed that we had either fucked at least once or that we did it regularly.

She was accused of "making pornos with that fat black dude" (me), and she and I found that shit to be hilarious. She was a confident woman, and we both had a comparable sense of humor that fed off each other.

At several points in time, her "baby daddy" seemed to become the world's most insecure person. He hurled ridiculous accusations at both of us, which seemed shocking at the time to me.

That's because parts of my confidence were chipped away by a subconscious tendency to perceive slim women as being out of my league. Yet somehow, her boyfriend saw it as not only a fleeting possibility that I was nailing his gal, but he also felt that it was guaranteed.

The greatness of that situation lies in the fact that he had far more belief in me than I had in myself. What in the hell was the universe trying to teach me from that moment?

My haters (secret admirers) already knew that I was the shit. Yes—they observed me and saw a guy who possessed what appeared to be surreal self-assurance, easily discernible intelligence, and a personality more engaging than a pair of infant twins batting their eyelashes!

You Possess Something That Others Wish They Had

Believe it or not, there are people in your life that either wish they had what you already have or wish they were you altogether. That sounds ridiculous, right? Don't be so quick to assume that you don't have anything someone else would want. I've always believed that we all have secret admirers—some are haters who are secretly envious of us, and some are friends, family, or acquaintances who simply wish that they possessed some of our qualities, or dare I say, swag?

One of the most common reasons you don't recognize admiration from others is that you are so used to your life, talents, natural gifts, and the "perks" that come with it. You usually ignore the pluses that you possess, or you may not even realize that certain things are considered desirable to others.

For years I took for granted my distinct ability to engage almost anyone in compelling conversations. To me, it was such a natural part of my personality since childhood that I never felt that it was an advantage or something that everyone didn't possess.

I later found out that it was an essential skill for anyone to have, yet not many people have it. I guarantee that you have qualities that are the envy of your "secret admirers." Just because you might be down on yourself or think that you are nothing special doesn't mean all other people share that belief!

Here are five common things that you have that your "secret admirers" almost certainly wish they did.

1. YOUR RELATIONSHIP WITH SOMEONE THEY ARE IN A RELATIONSHIP WITH

Back in high school, I was good friends with a girl that I saw all the time because she and I were in a couple of classes together. As the months passed, we became closer, and some people assumed we were "going steady." We wrote each other notes multiple times during the school day and gave them to each other between classes or in class.

I wanted us to be "more than friends," but I was too damn insecure to bring it up to her. She eventually started dating a guy who lived near her, which pissed me off. Ironically, he was jealous of my relationship with his girlfriend because she talked about me all the time. He also admitted to her that he wished that he could "write as well as" me after reading a few of the letters I had written to her.

Think about the relationships in your life. Who are you close with that has a significant other, but you can always seem to make laugh or feel good about themself? If you're not already aware of it, it's a virtual certainty that you have a "secret admirer" that wishes he or she has what you have with their partner.

It illustrates that we often cannot assess the awesome gifts that we possess because we are so used to them that we don't see them as anything special.

2. Your Aura

The world is filled with all types of people, and some of them are just plain dull or boring. Others are social butterflies and can capture the attention of everyone in any room they enter. Your secret admirers have seen that from you, and they are fucking jealous of that. Why wouldn't they be? When a particular person is getting tons of attention in a given place, there will always be one or two folks who want that for themselves.

That presence and unique energy is your aura, and it's definitely a superpower. You don't always have to be outgoing or extroverted to have a magnetic aura. You could be laid back with little to say, and that mysteriousness creates an aura too.

I've always been told that I have a way with words, and I have been very comfortable conversing with anyone with humor, relatability, and intellect. Those attributes prompted the owner of a sales agency to declare that I have "qualities that [the company] can't teach." In other words, either you're born with those qualities, or you're not.

If you don't believe that you have an aura, I suggest that you ask people closest to you. You may have one but don't realize it because it's so natural. I should warn you, though. Most people who have a notable aura are aware of that shit.

3. Your Friendships

An old girlfriend admitted to being jealous of my life-long friendship with my best friend, Jermaine. At the time, he and I were 25 years old and had been friends for about 22 of those years. My girl at the time had moved from place to place as a kid and rarely established consistent friendships. Whenever she got close to someone, her parents usually stole her joy and moved away from that friend.

Hearing my girlfriend talk about her envy for my relationship with Jermaine was mind-blowing because I had never known that type of jealousy to be a thing! He and I are still close, and because of hateful comments she made over the years, I've learned that pettiness knows no boundaries.

You don't have to have a lifelong friend for one of your secret admirers to wish they had friendships like you. Any good friendship has the power to piss off someone else who doesn't have that blessing in their life. I suggest you think about the friendships that you have, especially the close ones.

Ask yourself the tough question: is anyone in my life jealous of this friendship? When someone hurls insults and negative talk at one of your good friends, that is a tell-tale sign of jealousy. You don't realize that a good friendship is something that others might envy or even try to sabotage because friendship is a natural thing to you.

Beware of the secret admirers because their claws can come out when you least expect that shit.

4. YOUR STYLE

Speaking of Jermaine, from childhood through young adulthood, he was known to dress well. Whatever the latest fashion trend was, he usually wore it if it was stylish and to his liking. During the second half of the 1990s, brand names such as Tommy Hilfiger, Nautica, Perry Ellis, Guess, Timberland, Ralph Lauren, and Nike were insanely popular. Jermaine wore those styles often and looked great in the process.

But his spiffy style attracted a decent amount of hate and negative critiques of him. People labeled him "stuck up" and "arrogant" while accusing him of "thinking he [was] better than everybody." No one was closer to him than me, and I never got that impression of him. He wore what he liked and what he liked happened to be mega-popular and, in most cases, pricey.

I soon realized that he was the victim of jealous secret admirers who apparently had no other recourse than to "tear him down."

If you are a snazzy dresser or have an enviable style, I guarantee some people wish they had that. Your job is to not worry about their admiration or hater behavior; instead, count your blessings for having what you have—and carry yourself like a badass!

5. Your Life Circumstances

A woman I know had an annoying ass habit of bitching about other women who were married and had the luxury of being stay-at-home moms. She, on the other hand, was a single mom of two children who always had to work to support her children alone.

She is a classic example of a secret admirer who complains about your life circumstances, because she wishes it were her life. What pissed me off about her rantings was that she had the power to put herself into a similar situation but didn't because it doesn't come easy. She also didn't know the details of those women's lives; she simply judged what she saw on the surface.

Your life circumstances could be many things. Maybe you have a nice deck that allows you to entertain the many friends you have. Maybe you have no children, and you have the freedom to travel to kickass vacation destinations. Whatever the case, you don't need to toot your own horn because your secret admirers already know you're the shit!

Keep In Mind

- It's obvious that we all have insecurities, but it's not as clear that you have things that your secret admirers envy.

- Among the desires of your admirers is the relationship you have with their significant other.

- Your unique aura is another edge that you possess that others wish they had.

- Your friendships can cause jealousy in your secret admirers like you wouldn't believe.

- Your style and fashion sense will make envious people grit their teeth in frustration of not possessing the same.

- There's something about the circumstances of your life that others wish was their reality. Never be fooled by well-wishers because they might not be sincere.

Part II: How to F.U.C.K (Your Insecurities)

"True forgiveness is when you can say 'Thank you for that experience."

–Oprah Winfrey

Forgive Those Muthafuckas

Forgiveness is the very first step to F.U.C.K. your insecurities. And trust me, I realize that sometimes you don't want to forgive certain assholes. But in this case, it will help you become a better person capable of anything you put your mind to.

Your insecurities can feel like a thief in the night, hell-bent on stealing your joy and self-confidence. If you allow them to continue to push you around like a bully in a schoolyard, you will never have a moment of peace.

That's why I suggest that you forgive those muthafuckas for all the pain they have caused you over the years. If you're anything like me, they still cause you pain on some level, so forgiveness is more important than ever.

I met a young woman online, and before long, she invited me to meet her somewhere in public. It was almost 11 pm when she suggested we meet, and there was no way I was leaving the house at that time.

She ended up coming to my place, and once she showed up, it was obvious that she was in the market for some fucking. At one point, she even took her clothes off in my living room to show me her body.

We talked about all types of shit before I finally asked her what she considered to be "good sex." She told me that she liked it "hard and aggressive" and that the guy needs to have "a big dick."

Instantly, I felt a range of emotions highlighted by intense self-consciousness and massive insecurity. My cock is about the size of a lady bug's pocketbook, so I knew I was already disqualified with this broad.

I convinced myself that I wasn't even going to try to have sex with her to save myself a shit ton of humiliation. Once I took her to my bedroom, she was quick out of her clothes again, she masturbated, and I finger banged her to climax.

The entire time, I kept thinking about how I wanted to nail this chick but that I wouldn't unveil my unqualified ding-a-ling. In the aftermath of this ridiculous encounter, I felt real shame and embarrassment and didn't want to admit to myself that I allowed a comment about big dicks to cower me.

My insecurities were punching me in the face, and it was difficult to admit to myself. The key point that I'm making here is that I had to experience this situation to grow as a person. But I had two choices: dwell on that bullshit and be miserable or grow from it and forgive my insecurities!

I chose forgiveness, and as I analyzed everything, I learned more about myself than I thought was possible. I strongly advise that you do the same thing—forgive your insecurities for all the pain them fuckers have caused you. Here's the path to forgiveness:

1. WRITE DOWN HOW THE PAIN HAS AFFECTED YOU

This is necessary because you need to "face" the reality of your insecurities. Have they caused you to miss out on fun or important moments or opportunities? Have you ever been too afraid to approach someone for a date? Wanted to apply for a well-paying job and just couldn't bear the thought of being rejected? Write down the details of those situations.

2. WHAT HAVE YOU GAINED FROM YOUR MOMENTS OF INSECURITY?

Legendary motivational speaker Jim Rohn used to talk about people's tendency to "get through the day" and on to the next one. He suggested that it would be much better if we "got *from* the day" because there is always something meaningful or important that we can learn from every day's lessons and events. With that mindset, ask yourself what you have gained from your moments of insecurity. It may seem crazy or strange, but there is almost always a silver lining to any bullshit we endure, so that is what you need to find.

3. NEVER DWELL ON THEM

Your insecurities are there to help you if you approach them with the right mindset. Acknowledge them and forgive them but never dwell on them. Yes, you might be a fat ass or have a big ass nose or be disabled, or you might just believe everyone is better than you. Whatever the case, you can't allow insecurities to hold your mind and life hostage because they don't deserve to have that level of power.

Whenever I felt insecure about my bite-sized wiener, I never allowed that feeling to push me away from having hot fun with chicks. Hell, I didn't get to pick my ding-a-ling, so why should I let the words, opinions, and jokes about the muthafucka dominate my mind?

Ask yourself that question about any of your insecurities.

4. HIRE A PRO

Sometimes, we need professional intervention. If you have followed my suggestions to deal with your insecurities and still find yourself fucked up mentally, get your ass to a counselor or another trained individual to help you. That could work wonders for you and teach you a lot about yourself in the process. It's nothing to be ashamed of, and whatever you find out will serve you well going forward.

Keep In Mind

- Your insecurities can feel like a thief in the night, hellbent on stealing your joy and self-confidence. I suggest that you forgive those muthafuckas for all the pain they have caused you over the years.

- Write down how the pain of your insecurities has affected you over the years because you need to "face" their reality.

- Ask yourself what you have gained from your moments of insecurity. Be honest.

- Don't dwell on your insecurities because you can't allow them to hold your mind and life hostage because they don't deserve to have that level of power.

If you have followed my suggestions to deal with your insecurities and you still find yourself fucked up mentally, get your ass to a counselor or another trained individual to help you.

*"The most difficult thing in life
is to know yourself."*

–Thales

UNDERSTAND THE BULLSHIT

Understanding is the second step to *F.U.C.K. Your Insecurities*. You need to understand where the insecurities come from and why. The more you know about yourself, the easier it will be to move past a lot of the garbage holding you back. You might even find some of that crap from your past to be funny while using it as a transformative resource.

Personally, I love a good laugh. The kids in my classes over the years did, too—at my expense. Here are some of my favorite childhood experiences that are hilarious now but sucked at the time. They help me understand my present self.

I was just seven years old when I begged my mom to buy me a pair of fake leather pants so that I could pretend that I was Michael Jackson. When I put them on, they were skin-tight because I was "extra husky." After two weeks, the between-the-thighs area peeled like the face of an acne-riddled teenager from my thighs rubbing together while wearing those pants.

In fourth grade, my mom had difficulty finding decent-looking clothes for me in my size. My super caring grandmother had the brilliant idea to give me some clothes that belonged to my grandfather. That was bad enough, but the clothes were from the 1970s, and I was a kid in late 1980s America. I was forced to wear a pair of lime green pants to school and got laughed at so hard, I felt like a circus clown.

The point is, I now understand where my insecurities come from; many years of being "the elephant in the room" while the media and general public romanticized "the skinny life." It was always a thorn in my side to literally not "fit in" while other kids were "normal," but I'm much better off now because of that.

Below is the process to understanding where your insecurities come from and how to adjust accordingly.

1. Revisit Your Past

Get some time alone if you need it to do some deep thinking about your past. When do you remember first feeling insecure about anything? This could be a time when you might've been scared to talk to a parent as a kid, or a friend made you feel insecure because you believed they were better than you, luckier than you, or even better looking than you.

Your feelings of insecurity could have come from bad grades in school, not getting a summer job that you wanted, or anything else that made you feel less than or "not good enough." This is all about excavating your past to understand the existence of your insecurities.

Before you can make progress against them, you need to be well informed on how they have worked against you all this time. As I mentioned, my insecurities took root because of me being a fat ass in a world built for skinny people. I suggest writing down what you come up with and leave nothing unsaid. No one will ever need to know what you write if you don't want them to.

2. CONSIDER HOW YOUR INSECURITIES HAVE HELD YOU BACK

This is another chance for you to get very honest with yourself. Think about all the crap that made you feel inferior, not good enough, or heightened your insecurities. Think about specific moments and whatever negative emotions you might've felt at the time and beyond.

Is there anything that you chose not to do for fear of failure? That is one of the biggest and most common forms of insecurity among us humans, so you're not a weirdo! Again, I suggest making a list of as many moments you can remember. A moment for me in which my insecurities held me back was during my entire senior year in high school.

I believed that no girl would give me the time of day and be my date for the prom because I had never had success with any girl before then. So, I didn't even try because I feared rejection or worse—being laughed out of the damn school. I also chose to disregard almost all senior activities because I was wrought with self-consciousness.

3. Discover Your Self-Worth

This will come as a surprise, but your self-worth is always in existence and constantly expanding. Your awareness of it is what fluctuates, so the important thing to do is to discover it. Your self-worth makes you priceless because it consists of all the things you like about yourself, your positive impact on people you've met, and the people who love you or enjoy your company.

Since your birth, you have contributed tons of value to the world that you can't comprehend. The kid you might have stood up for in grade school. The smile you put on a stranger's face while you both were standing in line at the grocery store ten years ago. The shoulder you gave for a friend to cry on when they were going through a fucked up time in their life.

The children you have raised, taught, or given birth to or—all of the above. The qualities that you possess that others have complimented multiple times. The advice you gave to others when they needed it or didn't want it but still needed it. This is your self-worth, and it's important to deal with your insecurities to even things out.

You're busy feeling insecure about things that you believe are out of your reach, or that someone has more than you or is better than you. But being aware of your self-worth puts it all in proper perspective! I was never aware of my self-worth over the years, and as far as I knew I was just a fat ass who was really funny and loved Michael Jackson and the TV show *Knight Rider*. I later realized that my loved ones were crazy about me and my daughters are in this world partly because of myself, and those things alone make me a very important person—and exceeded my insecurities by a ton. List the things that make up your self-worth, and you'll be well on your way to discovering value within yourself that will never go away. One key thing to remember: no matter how YOU feel about yourself, there are people in this world who not only like and love you but whose lives would not be the same (in a positive fashion) without having crossed your path. So never let a bad day or emotions block your understanding of your incredible value.

4. Your Spectacular 3

You need to get well acquainted with the wealth of amazing shit about you. You've been ignoring it for way too long, so now it's long overdue for you to make a short but very important list. This will require more thinking, but it's so worth it. Based on your knowledge of yourself and the lifetime of comments and compliments you've received, what three spectacular qualities do you possess?

Don't be afraid to brag about yourself because you are trying to get better acquainted with who you actually are.

As an example, my three spectacular qualities are my ability to make almost anyone laugh, make people feel good about themselves, and engage any person in interesting conversations. It took me years to realize that not everyone can do those things, and they have given me significant advantages in critical situations. If you are struggling to come up with your three, ask people who have known you for a decent amount of time what they like most about you. Think of situations that you've been a part of where your signature qualities came out.

Maybe you are a great listener, speaker, or perhaps you have a good bedside manner or can be empathetic effortlessly. I also encourage you to think of more than three if you choose. The point is to prove to yourself that you have so many wonderful things to offer the world that you've brought to the table for a long while. Remember, the people you might envy or believe to be better than you don't possess what you do.

5. ADJUST HOW YOU SHOW UP IN THE WORLD

Once you do the following, you should understand yourself much better:

- Take a complete inventory of your insecurities and where they come from
- Remember how they have held you back,
- Become aware of your self-worth
- List your three spectacular qualities.

This is self-discovery, which we all need, and I've learned a ton about myself the past couple of years.

Now, your mission is to adjust how you show up in the world. Hold on, though! This won't be some easy ass shit to implement, and there's no magic involved. As with anything, it will require patience and consistent practice to execute properly, but it's worth it. Showing up differently in the world means that you are fully aware that you will always have insecurities, but you will also be a kickass rock star in your own right, and no one can touch you.

You'll see your insecurities as a big part of your strength, and that will fuel your acceptance of them. Your self-worth proves that you are a priceless asset to this world and your three spectacular qualities will make you shine above others who wish that they had what you do. With all that knowledge, you just have to rinse and repeat over and over, and you will end up with far more self-belief than you've ever had.

Keep In Mind

- You need to understand where your insecurities come from and why.

- Get some time alone if needed to do some deep thinking about your past. When do you remember first feeling insecure about anything?

- Think about all the crap that made you feel inferior, not good enough, or just heightened your insecurities.

- Discover your self-worth. It is always in existence and constantly expanding.

- You need to get well acquainted with the wealth of amazing shit about you.

- Adjust how you show up in the world. You'll see your insecurities as a big part of your strength, and that will fuel your acceptance of them.

"Ever accidently throw something away and then later realize you actually needed it? Haha I did this with my life!"

–Unknown

CONFESS LIKE O.J. SHOULD'VE

Confession is the third step to F.*U.C.K. your insecurities.* When you keep your insecurities bottled up inside, you haven't truly faced them and stripped them of their power. I'm not telling you to walk into a room full of people and yell, "I'm ashamed of my big ass forehead," but I encourage you to integrate it smoothly into social conversations.

Guess what's more embarrassing than telling someone that you're insecure?

Pretending that you're not insecure! You're probably one of those people that act like you're confident and got your shit together, right?

Okay, that's a damn assumption, but it's probably not far from the truth. Let me tell you as directly as I can... when you confess your insecurities to people, not only does it show how fucking strong you are, but it gives you more freedom than skipping the underwear and free-balling it all day.

THE POWER OF
SELF DEPRECATION

My dictionary app defines self-deprecation this way:

"Belittling or undervaluing oneself;
excessively modest."

Have I ever looked down on myself? Hell yeah. Have I ever had low self-esteem, been insecure or self-conscious? Yes, to all of the above. I also happen to still be self-conscious and insecure.

Confessing your insecurities is one of the strongest things ever.

If you happen to be someone that pokes fun at yourself, I salute you. But there is a right way to do it and a wrong way to do it. The right way is the ultimate flex; the wrong way makes you look more ridiculous than Peter Griffin wearing a strapless dress.

THE INCORRECT WAY TO SELF-DEPRECATE

You really see yourself as mediocre, irredeemable, and useless. Other people are better than you, have more luck or advantages than you (in your mind). You are a walking pity party.

"If I wasn't so poor, then maybe I could live in a nicer place," you'd say about yourself.

I'm here to tell you, that's a losing strategy, and you're just inviting more pain into your life. There's always a better way.

THE CORRECT WAY TO SELF-DEPRECATE

You are very self-aware of how the public might perceive you. You know that you have flaws, shortcomings, and have made mistakes. But you're also very aware of your awesome qualities and the fact that no one else is without their own "lousy crap."

"I might be broke as hell, but I still have a roof over my head. Even though my car has more miles on it than a damn space shuttle, it gets me where I need to go!"

In that example, you're acknowledging the less than wonderful aspects of your life. But you aren't making it a self-pity party out of it. You're owning your "mess" and still standing tall. Consider this classic line from an iconic hip-hop artist:

"Heart throb never, Black and ugly as ever, however,
I stay Coogi down to the socks.
Rings and watch filled with rocks.
And my jam knock in your Mitsubishi..."
–The Notorious B.I.G.

In less than thirty words, Biggie acknowledged his "perceived visual shortcomings" while subtly informing the listener that he was still a badass muthafucka because his clothes and jewelry were phenomenal, he had the cash to buy it, and he was truly winning because his music is playing in the listener's car. Flawless execution!

CHASE THE "RABBIT" STRATEGY

The film *8 Mile* perfectly illustrates how to confess your insecurities methodically—and with the swag of a certified badass.

Eminem's character B Rabbit advances to the final round of a battle rap competition by masterfully dismissing his opponents with clever puns and put-downs, earning him tons of respect and applause from the packed audience in attendance. But he uses an entirely different strategy for the final round because he had to go first, instead of going last as in previous rounds.

To everyone's surprise, B Rabbit forcefully cleans out his *own* closet by hurling insults at...himself. He took ownership of all the things that his rivals had ripped him for during the entire film. He told the predominantly black crowd, with surprising passion, that he is not only white, but he's also "a fucking bum" who lives in a "trailer with [his] mom." From there, he tells the crowd about his "dumb friend named Cheddar Bob who shoots himself in his leg with his own gun" and admits to having been jumped "by all six of you chumps."

By now, his recently defeated rivals appeared to be in a state of shock, but the crowd feels his searing energy and is vibing with him. He closes his unexpected master stroke with a flourish, "I'm a piece of fucking white trash; I say it proudly…here, tell these people something they don't know about me."

At that moment, he tosses the mic to his almost catatonic opponent, so that he can have his turn. The crowd cheers wildly.

First, I completely understand that this is a movie, but it is far from being *just* a movie. I have used this type of unimpeachable strategy many times, and I feel that everyone should adopt this method of self-love by way of confession. To me, it becomes much easier to make peace with your perceived shortcomings when you have not allowed them to define you.

I could easily make the case that B Rabbit's so-called shortcomings didn't define him. Yes, he was white and poor, but he was also an employed man who stood up to his mom's abusive boyfriend. He was also an awesome big brother and proved it multiple times in the film as he kept his little sister safe. Sure, his one friend was an Uncle Tom, and one of his other friends shot himself accidentally, but none of that had anything to do with him. Also, those same friends always had his back.

Yes, he did get jumped, which is nothing to be ashamed of for the sheer fact that it wasn't a fair fight. If anything, it makes the people that jumped him look pathetic because they didn't fight one-on-one and make it an honest battle. Yes, his "traitor" and fake acquaintance had sex with the chick that was seen by some as being B Rabbit's girl, but that says more about her whorish ways than anything about him. Also, Rabbit could just as easily go and fuck someone else's girl, including one of theirs. And there was never a point in the film when he explicitly stated that she was his "girl" anyway.

By embracing your "flaws" and "shortcomings," you take ownership of all aspects of yourself. None of those things make you a bad person or less than a person. I have encouraged people to make fat jokes at my expense because I'd rather have people be "real" to my face instead of fake. Plus, many of the jokes are absolutely hilarious to me.

Knowing Your Self-Worth Makes Confession Easy

When you truly understand your value based on your self-worth, confessing your "shortcomings" and "flaws" suddenly becomes the easiest shit in the world to do. In the midst of all that, you'll also be fully aware that everyone on the planet has flaws and insecurities too.

If you are a talented musician, an interior decorator, or own a profitable construction company, you are blessed. Let's say you also have a loving wife and two amazing young children—and live in a nice house. Now, imagine someone (a rival) comes along and calls you a loser because you don't have a master's degree, but they do. They happen to know that you're insecure about not having that "lofty" college degree, so they poke at you.

"Being a loser never felt so damn good," you could say. "Who would've thought that a guy with a goddamn high school diploma could run his own business and have a beautiful family *and* own a home? I feel bad for the idiots that blew all their student loan money on a worthless degree!"

That is how you confess your insecurities like a badass.

KEEP IN MIND

- Confessing your insecurities is one of the strongest things ever.

- There is a right and wrong way to self-deprecate.

- Use the same "confession" strategy that Eminem used in the film *8 Mile*.

- Knowing your self-worth makes confession easy.

*"If you can't fly, run. If you can't run then walk,
If you can't walk, crawl, but whatever you do...
Keep moving."*

–Dr. Martin Luther King, Jr.

KICK THEM BITCHES TO THE SIDE AND KEEP MOVING

The fourth and final step to *F.U.C.K. your insecurities* is "kick" —as in kick them bitches to the side and keep moving! You ain't got the time to dwell on them and stew in a pool of your own tears. You must show those bitches (insecurities) who's the boss.

I'm guessing that you think you need more confidence to overcome your insecurities, right? I'm here to tell you that confidence is bullshit because it comes and goes, and you can't control when the hell it'll come knocking.

I am a firm believer that you can and should use yourself and the powerful stories of others to kick your insecurities to the side and keep moving. Think of it this way: if they pulled off amazing shit in their life, I'm sure they had their own insecurities to deal with.

That means you can do the same.

13 REASONS WHY YOU CAN JUMP OVER YOUR INSECURITIES AND KICK ASS IN LIFE

1. You've overcome difficult shit many times in the past.

2. You bring something unique to the table that no one else does.

3. Oprah Winfrey overcame poverty, teen pregnancy, and abusive relationships to become the first Black female billionaire in history.

4. LeBron James overcame a single parent household and a poverty-stricken life to become a legendary professional athlete and businessman.

5. JAY-Z overcame a single parent household, living in a dangerous housing project, and a drug dealing past to become a multi-platinum recording artist, multi-time award winner and a billionaire businessman.

6. Barack Obama overcame his ethnicity in a long-standing racially divided country to become the first black president in the history of the United States.

7. Your life experiences give you an original perspective that can be channeled into something of massive value for other people.

8. Self-doubt and limiting beliefs are normal and natural emotions, and everyone, including wealthy legends, has them.

9. Resistance is a huge part of accomplishing anything significant. When you feel it, you're on the right track.

10. You don't have to feel confident, ready, or worthy to try something that's intimidating. Confidence is overrated, and courage is far more important.

11. Passion and consistency will allow you to outlast anything and anyone else. It is natural to overestimate others and underestimate yourself. You have more power than you think, just stay the course.

12. You overcame your biggest odds at the time of conception. Just becoming a human being requires literally beating hundreds of billions of odds. When you beat out all other sperm, you proved your own incredible resilience.

13. You are your own worst critic, meaning that you probably overlook a lot of your important attributes. You have what it takes right now! No other tool or advice is needed. Just start whatever you are aiming for.

KEEP IN MIND

You are far more powerful than you think, and your insecurities are at a distinct disadvantage in dealing with you. When it comes to them, your thoughts should be "I came. I saw. I conquered."

PART III: HOW TO BE THE BEST IN THE WORLD

"The only one who gets to decide your worth is you. It doesn't come from your bank account or the number of friends you have. It doesn't come from what someone else says you are worth. It's called self-worth for a reason—it comes from you. It comes from being yourself and being proud of who you are. It comes from being someone that you can count on and someone you love. The numbers will change with time, but what won't change is who you are deep inside—beautiful, limitless, wonderful, creative, strong, capable—and that is where your worth comes from."

–Nikki Banas

WHAT A HUNDRED BILLION DOLLARS CAN'T BUY

The world in which we live has a bunch of filthy rich ass people who can have anything that money can buy. The filthiest of the rich can purchase any car, airplane, super yacht, home, or even island that they want.

But no amount of money, not even a hundred billion dollars, will ever be able to buy the most important thing that you possess: your self-worth.

It is a lot more valuable and essential than confidence and self-esteem because they come and go. As I said in an earlier chapter, your self-worth is always there; your awareness of it fluctuates. Understanding this simple idea will make all the difference in the world as you go through each day. Many of us look at people of means—the rich and wealthy, or whoever has more material things than us as being special or exclusive. I have come to realize that self-worth is more important than net worth. In fact, it is the most important thing there is.

KOBE'S LEGACY HAS NOTHING TO DO WITH MONEY

One of the most recent examples of the importance of self-worth vs. net worth is Kobe Bryant. I was one of the millions of people around the world devastated by his sudden demise in January 2020, along with his 13-year old daughter and seven others. What struck me so much was that the vast majority of people who mourned him did so for all of the amazing things that he accomplished in his career and life. His enormous wealth was an afterthought at best.

There were constant appraisals of his basketball prowess, relentless work ethic and intensity, achievements in professional sports, and the life he was building in retirement. That life included books, coaching and mentorship to young NBA players; not to mention a media empire that was poised to create a wealth of content in the years to come.

Bryant was hailed as a strong and credible advocate for women's basketball and had begun outwardly championing the WNBA and women's college basketball. His daughter was his number one focus in building her up to become an eventual star in the game.

Nowhere in all of that post-mortem praise for Kobe was there any mention of him losing out on a gigantic net worth that ranks into the $400 million range. Nothing about his sprawling estate in an elite section of Los Angeles, his expensive vehicles, or anything materialistic.

There was endless talk of his development into a "girl dad," a man blessed with four beautiful daughters and a wife of close to 20 years. In the end, his self-worth, meaning the things that mattered the most yet cost nothing, were the most important. Nobody gave a fuck about the material shit.

The lesson in that is profound.

Focus on Your Ultimate Value

Somewhere along the line, you have struggled with being aware of your self-worth. That consists of the impact you have made upon the people who have crossed your path who love you, whether they are your parents or children, friends or acquaintances.

Your self-worth is also comprised of the singular gifts that you share with people: your ability to make people laugh, educate them, lift them up, and provide empathy.

Also, the talents you possess, your ability to make people feel good about themselves, connecting with people, or anything positive that you help people understand or believe in are all examples of your self-worth.

You certainly possess it, and it never leaves you. As the Kobe situation proved, it is far more valuable than your net worth. It is absolutely irreplaceable.

My advice is to focus on what you contribute to the people in your life, and the people who pass through your orbit. It is where your true value lives.

KEEP IN MIND

- Self-worth is a lot more valuable and important than confidence and self-esteem because they come and go.

- Self-worth is far more important than net worth.

- Kobe Bryant is one of the best examples of this as illustrated by the constant appraisals of his basketball prowess, relentless work ethic and intensity, achievements in professional sports, and the life he was building in retirement.

- Your self-worth is comprised of your singular gifts that you share with people.

- Focus on what you contribute to the people in your life, and the people who pass through your orbit. It is where your true value lives.

"Nobody built like you, you designed yourself."

—JAY-Z

THE GREATEST PRODUCT EVER CREATED

If you look in the mirror every day for one month and say ten times with conviction, "I am the greatest product ever created," you will eventually transform into an untouchable force of nature with unlimited potential.

During my career as a life insurance agent, the management was second to none. No matter what shortcomings I felt the company might have had, I ultimately learned the most enduring lessons from the coaching and workshops that our group would regularly receive.

One of the most pivotal lessons was about sales on a fundamental level. From the very beginning of my tenure with the company, we were told that sales is nothing more than "the transfer of belief."

The more I thought about it, the more it made so much sense. We were selling life insurance, and we were trained to think highly of our products. That way, we could speak enthusiastically about them to potential customers.

1. THINK OF YOURSELF AS A GREAT PRODUCT THAT YOU BELIEVE IN

The exact same thing applies to all of us as people. Whenever you present yourself in job interviews, as a parent, as a potential date, or whatever the case might be, you are your own best product.

You should be enthusiastic about what you have to offer in any situation. If you are genuine, your enthusiasm will ultimately transfer to whoever you're trying to "sell."

That is the transfer of belief.

I'm still a work in progress on this, though I've made strides forward. I believe this could be incredibly useful for you if you struggle with self-esteem or limiting beliefs. We tend to overthink situations and look down on ourselves.

2. STOP ELEVATING OTHERS AND MINIMIZING YOURSELF

Many of us tend to elevate other people and minimize ourselves, meaning we are transferring that belief to the other person or situation, which is exactly what we should never do.

For years, I looked at some females as being "out of my league," which is a ridiculous thing to think. Never do that with anyone. I don't give a damn if she's so "out of this world" that she's the CEO of NASA! No matter what the other person thinks or what may be true, know that what you have to offer is more than enough. Hell, it might even be spectacular!

You have unique and valuable attributes, and those are some of the things that can uplift your view of yourself. Then, you could transfer that positive belief in yourself to the situations that call for it.

When you don't do this and instead act as though you are not good enough or worthy enough or behave as though someone or something is out of your league, you are being crushed by those annoying ass self-limiting beliefs.

Translation: you are then transferring those limiting beliefs about yourself to others. They see you devaluing yourself, so you are seen as a devalued person.

3. BE MINDFUL OF YOUR AURA AND SELF PRESENTATION

Be mindful as much as you can to move through life with the aura and self-presentation that positively speaks for you.

You believe in yourself because no one in the world is better than you, and no one could ever be you. That is the belief you need to transfer to other people and situations.

And believe me, I'm working on myself with this daily because it sucks to feel limited and inferior to other people when we are all just people. We have strengths and weaknesses, no matter who the hell we are—rich and famous, or poor and unknown.

Golden advice: keep believing in your best product, which is you—and transfer that belief to everyone who crosses your path because you are the greatest product ever created!

Keep In Mind

- Sales is the transfer of belief, and you are selling yourself every day.

- You should be enthusiastic about what you have to offer in whatever situation.

- We sometimes tend to elevate others and minimize ourselves, meaning we are transferring that belief to the other person or situation, which is exactly what we should never do.

- You have unique and valuable attributes, and those are some of the things that can uplift your view of yourself.

- You believe in yourself because no one in the world is better than you, and no one could ever be you. That is the belief that you need to transfer to other people and situations.

*"The real difficulty is to overcome how
you think about yourself."*

—Maya Angelou

How to Write the Ultimate Love Letter—To Yourself

If we can pleasure ourselves, we can certainly write a love letter to ourselves.

Self-love is a form of self-compassion. According to the Emily Program, here are a few ways that it will benefit us:

- Greater happiness

- Stronger resilience

- Increased motivation

- Better physical and mental health

I'm really good at writing letters to women that I like. That could be "like" as in "I really dig their vibe," or "like" as in "I want to navigate the inside of their panties," or even "like" as in "I really love them." I think many of us are good at conveying how we feel about special people in our lives.

Except, we don't always seem to be good at expressing love to ourselves. At least, that's how it had been for me many times since I made my world premiere that April Fool's Day many moons ago.

Nowadays, I am damn good at expressing self-love, and I am about to explain how you can get better at expressing how much you love yourself.

"Everyone of us needs to show how much we care for each other and, in the process, care for ourselves."

—Diana, Princess of Wales

BEFORE YOU WRITE IT, GET CLEAR ON WHAT'S WONDERFUL ABOUT YOU

Believe it or not, a love letter works wonders. Yup. A love letter to yourself. Think about how many times you have called yourself "dumb" or "stupid" without even flinching.

You need to stop that nonsense.

One time, I called myself an idiot because I started French kissing a girl before taking my damn gum out of my mouth. It was ridiculous.

Writing a love letter to yourself can only happen after discovering your self-worth and the things you really like or appreciate about yourself. Brainstorm ideas on paper or in a note-taking app. Then, convert the ideas into a list.

BE YOUR BIGGEST FAN WHEN WRITING TO YOURSELF

Do not overthink it; perfection is not a requirement. Complete the rough draft of the list and start writing the letter to yourself. Flatter yourself. Hell, get mushy if you prefer. This is for your eyes only.

Even if you think you suck, I guarantee there's some shit you also think is wonderful about yourself and very likely love without realizing it.

For example, if you have functioning legs, you love them. That might seem like a silly or strange thing to include, but if you saw a person in a wheelchair, your perspective might change.

In that respect, being able to walk is an extraordinary quality to have.

So, put that in the letter if you are struggling to think of other stuff. I'll give you a couple of examples that I wrote in my love letter to myself.

1. I mentioned how much I appreciate my incredible sense of humor.

2. I talked about how much I love the way that I lift other people up when they are not feeling their best.

Copy my ideas if the shit sounds good to you.

I mentioned how much I love that I have grown so much as a person over the years. There is no limit to what you can write.

The whole point is to get rid of negative self-talk and gradually move towards feeling much better about yourself.

Face it; you are a special commodity in some way, shape, or form. You should celebrate that.

KEEP IN MIND

- One of the most important relationships you can ever have is the one you have with yourself.

- Remember how fucking amazing you are! Practice saying it out loud to yourself because it needs to become a non-negotiable self-belief.

- Look at your perceived flaws and shortcomings and still understand just how valuable you are.

- The rest of the world tears you down enough. We all have enemies or jealous people or some form of haters. Some we know about, some are secret. Whatever the case, you must be your own cheerleader. Sometimes that might mean being your own 'secret admirer,' but in a positive way.

- Write that letter to yourself, and read it as often as needed.

"Courage is not having the strength to go on; it's going on when you don't have the strength."–Theodore Roosevelt

CONFIDENCE AIN'T SHIT. COURAGE RULES THE WORLD

More scared than the Tin Man approaching the Wizard, I asked a smart and sophisticated black woman for a kiss. She served up her answer as straight as a glass of vodka—neat.

"I don't want to kiss you," she said, with no fucks given.

For the record, I'm a black guy who's never kissed a sista' before. A friend of mine referred to her as "a prized woman." Shit, I couldn't be mad at her.

The sun didn't fall out of the sky. My daughter didn't block me on her phone. And I'm still a self-made sex symbol.

In other words, being told 'no' ain't that damn serious. I'll live.

I am amazed at how strong of a grip that fear has over us. I'm not talking about a fear of dying or fear of a monster. I'm talking about the fear of going after something that we want.

We act as if Jason Vorhees is chasing us. We avoid taking on challenges.

I have long been the ringleader of being scared as shit of trying to do intimidating crap that matters to me.

Enough of that weak B.S. This mindset has been modified to battle that monster known as fear, and I want you to feel the same fucking way.

You need to stop assuming that you have to be confident before trying to do something that matters to you.

Get this through your fucking head—confidence is temporary. Courage is one of your most reliable assets. You will not always feel confident going into a situation, but you can summon courage at a moment's notice and jump right in.

There is a natural fear associated with trying to succeed at anything. We believe that confidence is required to make our dreams come true, but courage is far more essential in those situations.

When you are nervous, scared, or insecure, you can't really help those emotions. But courage pulls you up by your bootstraps and leads you towards the goal. When your belief is strong enough, you can overcome fear and insecurity with courage.

THE WORST-CASE SCENARIO IS NOT A BIG DEAL

I get it. It's embarrassing to fail at something or to be rejected by someone, especially when other people are around to see that shit. But you need to understand that there's no shame in trying something that does not go your way. Bestselling author and podcaster, Seth Godin, is fond of saying, "This might not work." That's a simple, yet wonderful way of thinking because the worst-case scenario if we "fail" or receive a "no" is really not that big of a deal.

Adopting that mindset will go a long way in transforming you into an unstoppable force of nature because people that are scared to fail are also afraid to try. A few years ago, I applied for a job online that I knew was a great opportunity. It required taking a personal assessment test, which didn't seem like a big deal, so I did it. I failed the assessment and received an email telling me that there were "better-qualified people" for that job.

It was very upsetting, but life moved on. Less than four months later, I applied with the same company (at the encouragement of a friend) and took the same assessment, though admittedly nervous as hell. Since my previous application, I learned one critical thing about taking assessments, which I applied the second time.

Long story short, I passed the exam and was brought in for an interview that went so well, it lasted nearly an hour longer than planned. Weeks later, the company hired me, and the experiences that I acquired from the entire process forever impacted my life in important ways. The easiest thing for me would have been to not try again after that initial rejection.

I knew that if I were to apply again, the worst possible outcome would have been another rejection, and that was something I could handle. I strongly urge you to think of the worst-case scenario in whatever you want to achieve. If you would like to ask a person on a date, but you are nervous as hell, what's the worst that could happen?

Being told "No" is about as horrible as it gets, and who gives a fuck? You already know your three spectacular qualities, so you could reframe a rejection as *them* missing out. If you want to apply for a job that you think might be out of your league, do it! The worst-case scenario is HR will ignore your application, tell you that you aren't qualified, or tell you they aren't hiring. There is nothing negatively life-changing about any of that, so why stress over it?

What Would You Do if You Knew You Would Fail?

This question is another gem from Godin. He spins off the famous question, "what would you do if you knew you wouldn't fail" into an even more fascinating one. What would you do if you knew you *would* fail? The beauty of this question is that it pinpoints the things you care most about, so in a sense, it serves as a filter for where you should focus your efforts if it's something important enough to you or not give a shit if it's small enough.

For instance, if I had failed the assessment again after applying for that job, nothing in my life would have been affected because I wasn't obsessed with the job. On the flip side, if I was obsessed with it, the possibility of getting to work there would have been significant enough for me to try at all costs despite the chance of failure. It's the main reason that millions of people play the lottery, especially when the jackpot is worth hundreds of millions of dollars.

The possibility of winning the lottery is slim to none, but that tiny chance is worth it to people to try, and the effort requires very little investment from anyone. Ask yourself what you would do or try if you knew you would fail. What outcome is important enough to you that the possibility of failure is irrelevant? What is something that you kind of want, but if you fail or get rejected, it's not the end of the world?

In my case, I desperately want to become a multi-time bestselling writer and even win awards for my work. I will certainly try to accomplish all that, but if I knew for a fact that I would fail at that shit, you better believe I'll still be writing my ass off! Your job is to find out what your thing is and get to work marching towards that because you are a star player!

How to Make Failure Impossible

There's only one way to make failure impossible: reframe your definition of success. The traditional thinking of what equals success is getting something you aim for: a job, a partner, a certain amount of weight loss, etc. But true success is overcoming your self-limiting beliefs, doubts, imposter syndrome, and of course, insecurities and still trying something.

Years ago, I stepped into the life insurance sales industry even though I wanted nothing to do with that kind of work. My cousin persuaded me to try it because of the enormous earning potential, so I reluctantly went along.

I went through months of training with endless ups and downs before eventually finding my footing and earning more money than ever before. In less than a year, my production dropped dramatically, and by the end of my time with the company, I was making practically no money.

I don't look back on that experience as a failure, even though I fell far short of my potential. I succeeded because I tried to do something that I actually hated, and I proved that I could execute the system and persuade people to buy the products. I began to falter because of an increase in laziness and disinterest in all that went into something that wasn't my destiny.

Even though I had tons of insecurities at the start and throughout, I kept moving forward, and that is how you make failure impossible. Your job is to make a list of two or three times that you felt you failed. Then, get clear with yourself on how there was no failure because trying and doing equated to success.

Keep In Mind

- Stop assuming that you must be confident before you try to do something that matters to you.

- Confidence is temporary. Courage is one of your most reliable assets. You will not always feel confident going into a situation, but you can summon courage at a moment's notice and jump right in.

- The worst-case scenario if you "fail" is not that big of a deal.

- What would you do if you knew you would fail? Do it!

- There's only one way to make failure impossible: re-frame your definition of success.

CLOSING THOUGHTS

I wrote this book because I want to put my more excruciatingly painful life experiences to good use. The best way to do that is to use them fuckers to help other people.

Being insecure can sometimes feel like a mental prison because, in some ways, you feel as though you're living to satisfy other people's view of what you "should be."

F.U.C.K. *Your Insecurities* is not just a book; it's a rallying cry. When you feel insecure, remember that it's normal shit and handle that nonsense the way I described in these pages.

The second, moment, or day that you discover your self-worth will be a monumental awakening for you. You'll realize that your insecurities and your courage can co-exist and positively serve you in ways you've never thought possible.

Do me a huge favor: promise to never dim your light to brighten someone else's. You are the greatest product ever created, and damn it, you better start acting like it.

I look forward to hearing about how you are pushing your insecurities to the side and showing up in the world like a badass.

Let's get together online! Twitter: @DeanteYoung Instagram: DeanteUnlimited

Facebook Group: F.U.C.K. Your Insecurities

And subscribe to my mailing list to read more about dealing with self-doubt, limiting beliefs, insecurities and all types of shit that I've learned through my life experiences and others.

Thanks again!

-D.Y.

THE END

www.ingramcontent.com/pod-product-compliance
Lightning Source LLC
Chambersburg PA
CBHW052139090426
42741CB00009B/2147